D0832821

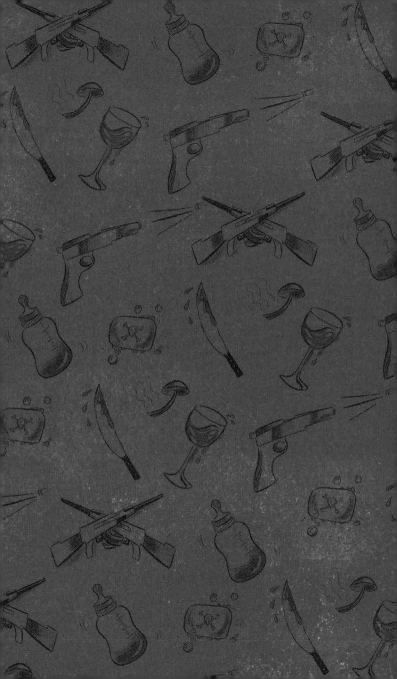

WOMEN Who KILL

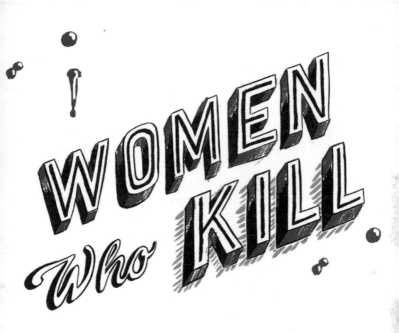

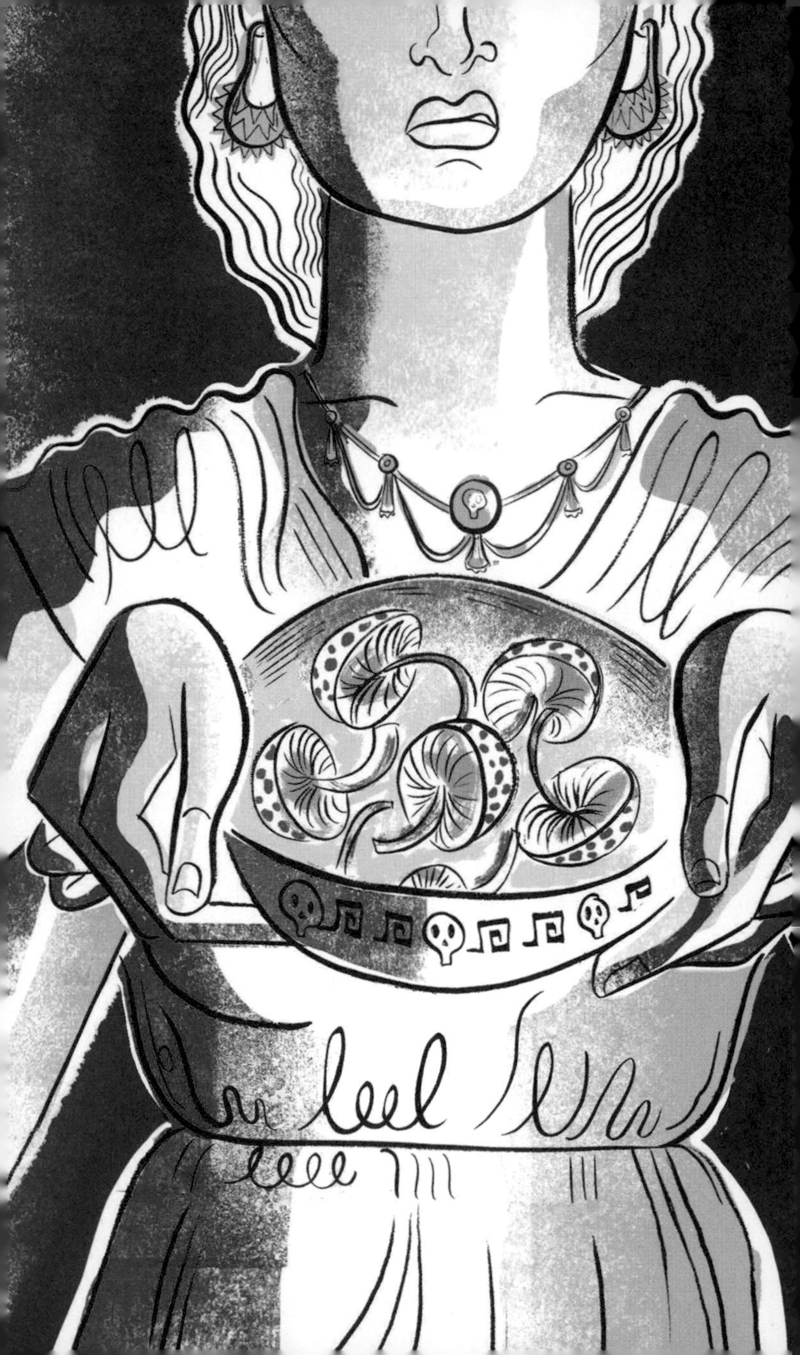

AGRIPPINA

Date of birth: 15 AD
Location: Italy
Date of murder: 54 AD
Methodology: Poison
Penalty: None

Agrippina was a notorious charismatic beauty of Ancient Roman aristocratic stock. Her cruel and impetuous brother, Caligula, became emperor of Rome in 37 AD. When he caught Agrippina plotting his assassination, he exiled her, separating her from her baby, Nero. The exile was lifted after Caligula was murdered and Agrippina's uncle, Claudius, replaced him.

Upon her return to Rome, Agrippina fostered a very close physical relationship with Claudius, who even referred to her in his speeches: "my daughter and foster child, born and bred, in my lap, so to speak". In the face of widespread disapproval at the incestuous nature of their relationship, Agrippina and Claudius were married.

Once she had assumed her position, Agrippina ruthlessly eliminated anyone who could possibly pose a threat to her or to Nero. This included Claudius's son, Britannicus, who she isolated from his father, persuading Claudius to appoint Nero instead as his successor. However, a few years later, Claudius repented, turning away from Agrippina and favouring Britannicus over Nero. Sensing his change of heart, Agrippina took action, feeding Claudius a plate of poisoned mushrooms at a banquet. Claudius died and Nero took the throne.

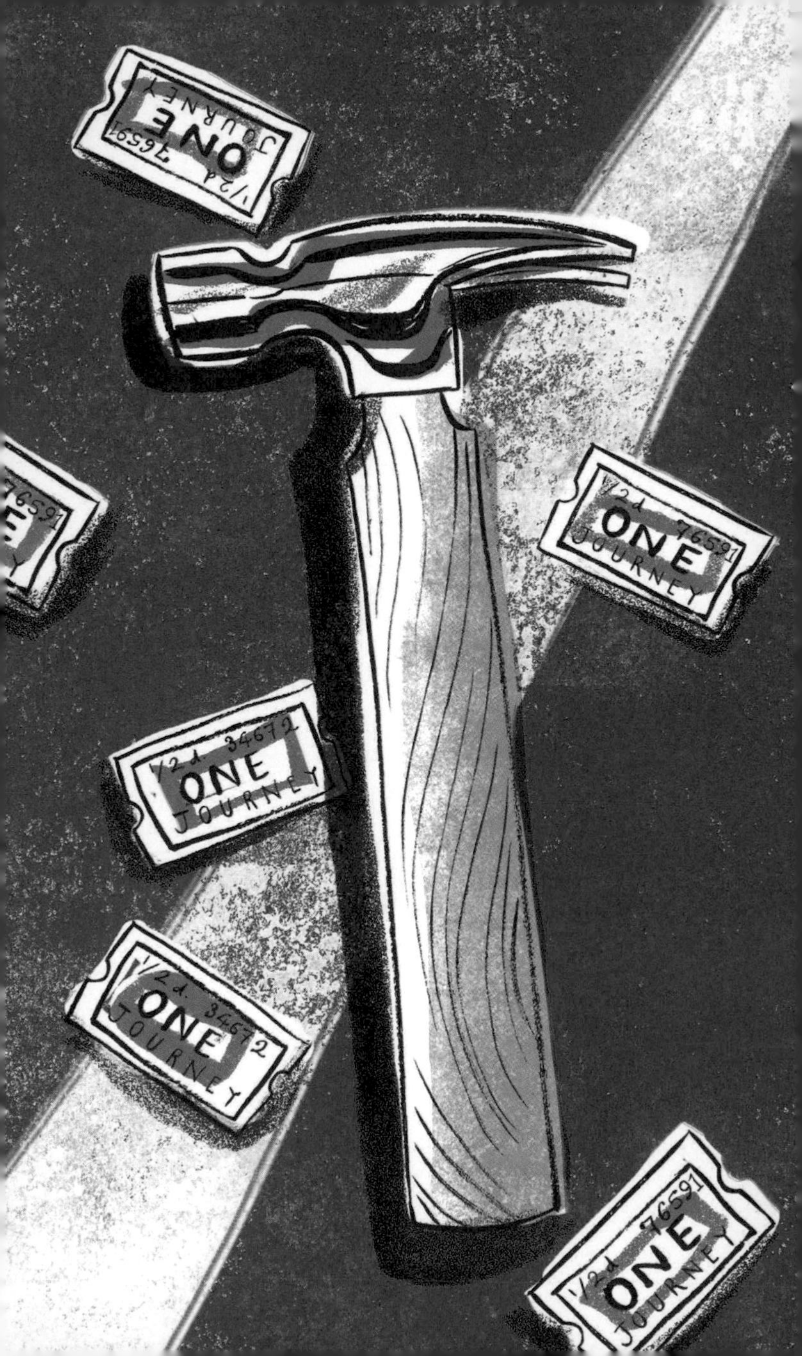
½d 76591 ONE JOURNEY
½d 76591 ONE JOURNEY
½d 34672 ONE JOURNEY
½d 34672 ONE JOURNEY
½d 76591 ONE JOURNEY

MARGARET ALLEN

Date of birth: 1904
Location: England
Date of murder: 1948
Methodology: Hammer
Penalty: Death by hanging

Margaret Allen was a transsexual in the days before such a term had been heard of. Born into a very large Lancashire family, Allen identified as a boy at a very young age, dressing in boys' clothing and eventually taking on jobs traditionally reserved for men; coal delivery, building work, and finally bus conducting. She cut her hair short, drank in working mens' clubs and called herself Bill.

Her mental state was fragile; she was prone to violent verbal and physical outbursts, and after the death of her mother, suffered severe depressions. According to a friend and possible lover, Annie Cook, Allen tried to take her own life on a number of occasions.

In August 1948, the body of Nancy Chadwick, an elderly, cantankerous neighbour, was found, her head stoved in and a trail of blood leading to Allen's door. Allen initially pretended to help the police investigation, but it quickly became apparent that she was the culprit. She confessed to killing Chadwick with the sharp end of a coal hammer. By way of explanation she simply stated "I was in one of my funny moods". Allen was hanged at Strangeways prison a month later, the first woman to be hanged in 12 years.

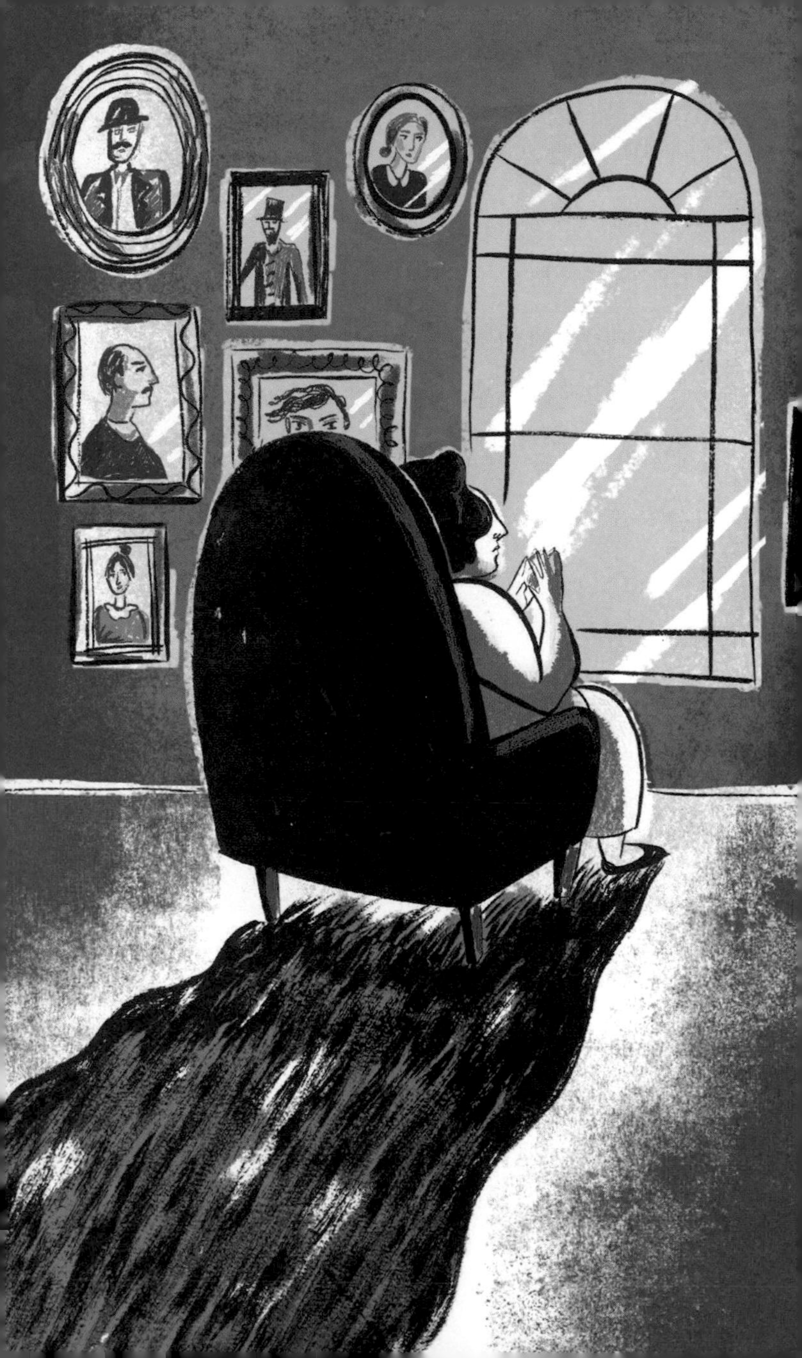

MA BARKER

Date of birth: 1873
Location: USA
Date of murders: 1932–1935
Methodology: Shooting
Penalty: Shot by FBI

Kate Barker was the mother of four unruly boys; Herman, Arthur, Lloyd and Fred. From a young age they were in and out of trouble with the law. In the spring of 1931, Fred was released from prison and brought home with him a fellow parolee, Alvin Karpis. The Barker brothers joined forces with the newcomer to form the Karpis-Barker gang, and used their mother's home in Tulsa as their hideout.

The gang planned a string of lucrative bank robberies, killing anyone who got in their way, including police. They then branched out into kidnapping, demanding huge ransoms for the release of their wealthy prisoners. In 1934, they kidnapped Edward Bremmer, who happened to be a friend of the president. It was a step too far. Over the following year, the FBI ensured that most of the gang members were killed or arrested. In January 1935, Fred and Ma Barker were killed in a shootout outside Ma Barker's cottage in Florida.

After the event, J Edgar Hoover labeled Ma Barker as the leader of the gang, describing her as "the most vicious, dangerous criminal brain of the last decade". However, evidence suggests that whilst she was aware of the crimes and reaped the rewards, she was probably not the mastermind we imagined.

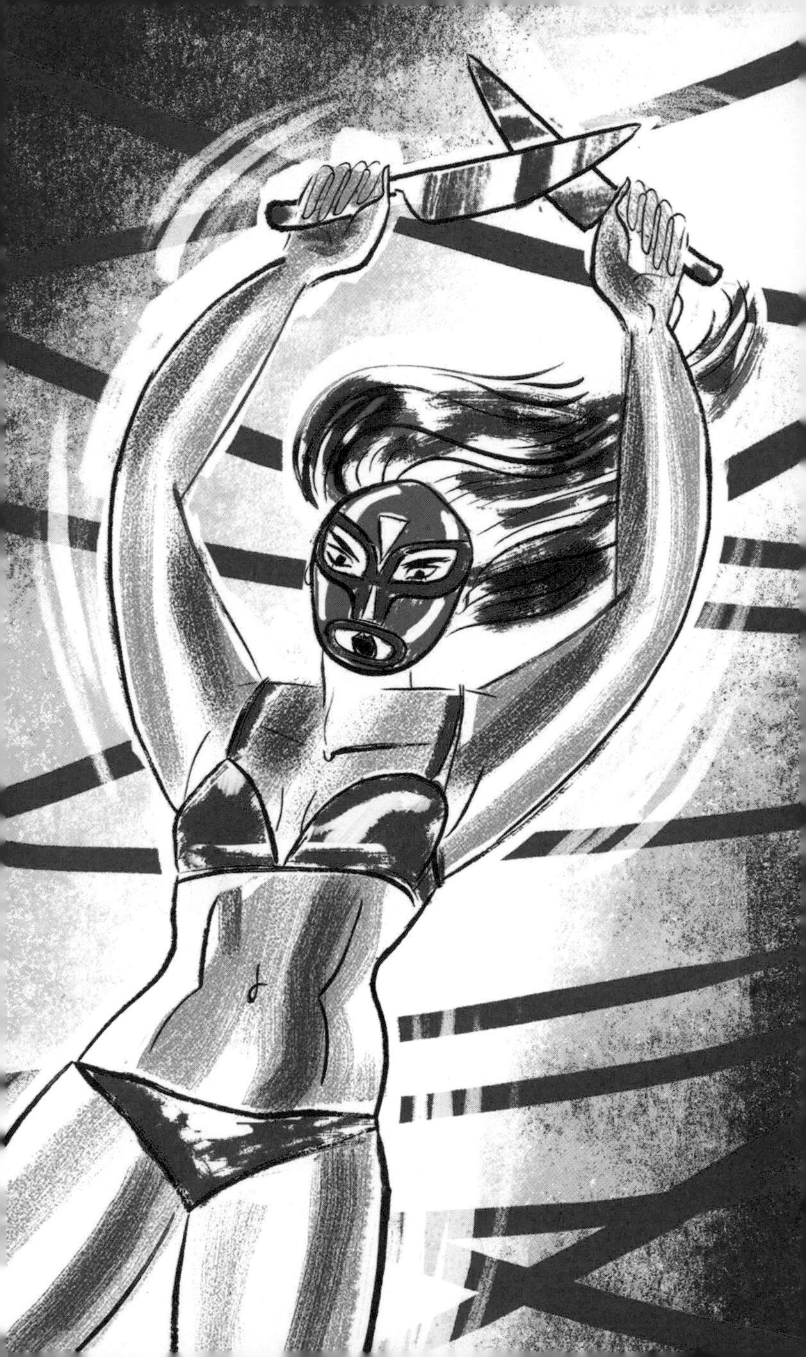

JUANA BARRAZA

Date of birth: 1957
Location: Mexico
Date of murders: 1990-2008
Methodology: Strangulation
Penalty: Sentenced to life

Juana Barraza was a colourful character. A semi-professional *lucha libre* wrestler known as 'The Silent Lady,' she had a prolific sideline in killing elderly women, thus earning herself a second epithet, *La Mataviejitas* or 'Little Old Lady Killer'. Offering to help with shopping bags or posing as a government official, Barraza gained her victims' trust, and then strangled them with objects such as phone cables, tights or a stethoscope, which she would carry around with her.

Barraza evaded capture for a long time, as Mexican police mistakenly assumed from witness accounts that they were hunting for a transvestite. Eventually, in 2006, she was caught when the lodger of a victim returned home early and found Barraza with the body of his 82-year-old landlady.

Barraza was linked by fingerprint evidence to 11 murders, but it is thought that her actual tally was around 48. She showed no remorse, telling the court that she was exacting revenge for a traumatic childhood, in which her mother sold her at the age of 12 to a man who abused her. She was found guilty on 16 charges of murder and was sentenced to 759 years in prison.

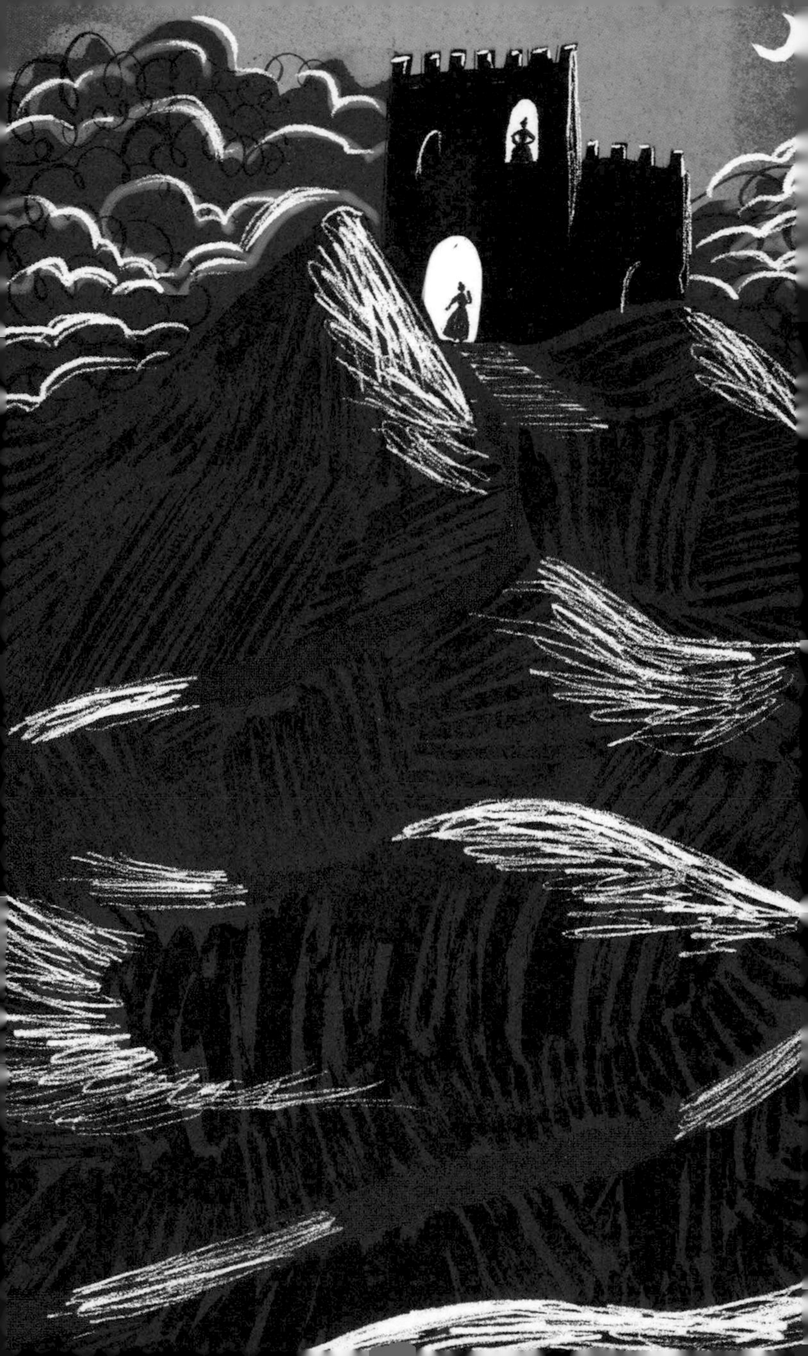

COUNTESS
ELIZABETH BATHORY

Date of birth: 1560
Location: Hungary
Date of murders: 1576–1600
Methodology: Various
Penalty: Confinement until death

Hungarian noblewoman, Elizabeth Bathory, was married at the age of 14 to Count Ferenc Nadasdy, and the two became known for their sadistic abuse of servants. When Nadasdy went to war, Bathory became ever more extreme in her antics. Convinced that only the blood of virgins would preserve her youth for her husband, she would lure peasant girls to her castle, kill them and bathe in their blood. Witnesses observed her biting, burning and torturing the girls with great relish.

After Nadasdy's death, Bathory sunk into a terrible depression, closing herself in her castle and demanding that girl after girl was brought to her to be tortured and eventually killed. Once she had exhausted the supply of local peasants, she turned to the lesser nobility. This proved a step too far, however, and the Hungarian king, who had thus far turned a blind eye due to Bathory's aristocratic standing, intervened. Soldiers stormed the castle, finding the grounds strewn with the bodies of hundreds of girls. Diary evidence indicates that Bathory was responsible for around 650 deaths.

Even so, Bathory escaped punishment. Whilst her assistants were executed, she was merely sentenced to spend the rest of her days in her bricked up castle.

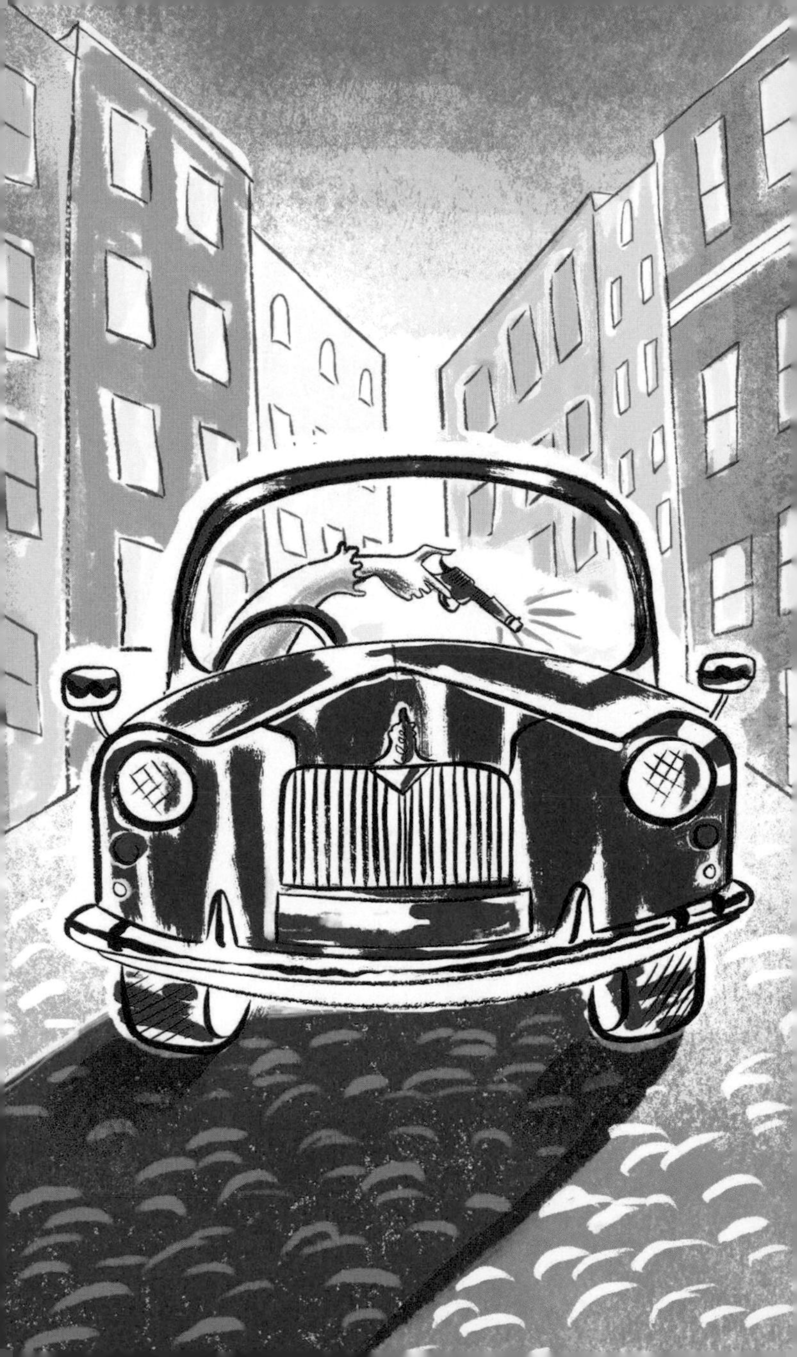

LINDA CALVEY

Date of birth: 1948
Location: England
Date of murder: 1990
Methodology: Shooting
Penalty: Sentenced to life

Linda Calvey was a part of the East London gangster scene of the '70s and '80s, fraternising with criminals such as Reggie Kray and Frankie Fraser. She became known as the 'Black Widow' because all of her lovers ended up either dead or behind bars.

After her first husband was shot by police, Calvey hooked up with another criminal, Ronnie Cook. In 1981, Cook was jailed for 16 years for his involvement in a robbery. When he came up for parole, Calvey was concerned that Cook would discover her various infidelities and so arranged for him to be killed. She paid hitman Danny Reece £10,000 to dispose of Cook whilst he was on day release. The plan literally misfired when Reece accidentally shot Cook in the elbow. Unable to finish the job, Reece handed the shotgun over to Calvey, who shouted "Kneel!", before blasting Cook at point blank range.

Despite their pleas of innocence, Calvey and Reece were both sentenced to life in prison. The two got married during their time inside, but later divorced. Calvey was released in 2009 after serving 18 years. At the time of her release Calvey was Britain's longest serving female prisoner.

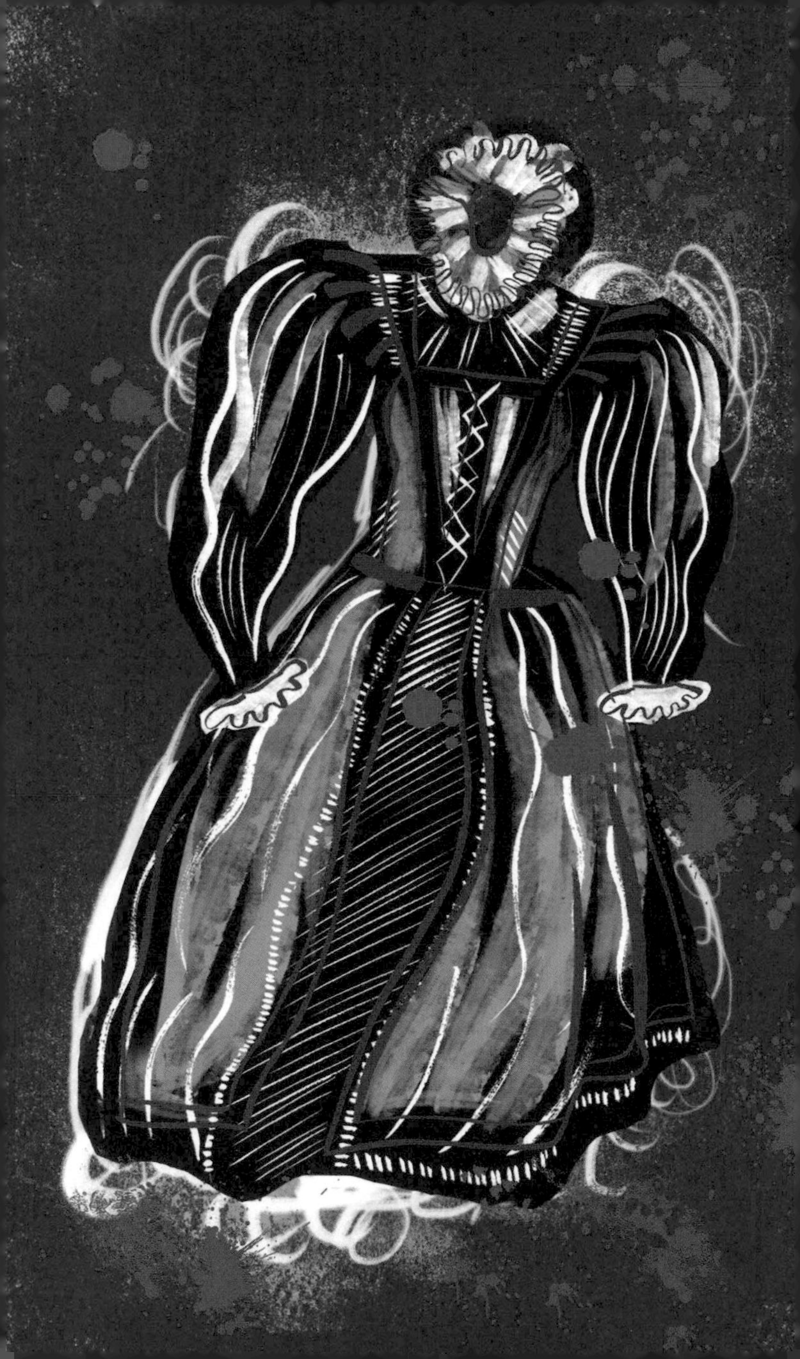

BEATRICE CENCI

Date of birth: 1577
Location: Italy
Date of murder: 1598
Methodology: Hammer
Penalty: Death by beheading

Beatrice Cenci was the daughter of cruel and wealthy nobleman, Francesco Cenci. His depraved acts were known around Rome; he was convicted of forcing his mistress to commit sexual acts against her will, of molesting young boys and of starving his servants. His acts of cruelty extended to his children, and he raped Beatrice repeatedly.

Beatrice reported her father to the authorities, but they did nothing. When he learned of her betrayal, Francesco sent Beatrice, along with her stepmother, Lucrezia, and her two brothers to his country estate, where they were effectively imprisoned and tortured. With the help of two servants, the four Cencis attempted to poison Francesco with drug-laced wine. This had no effect, so they bludgeoned him to death with a hammer and threw his body over the balcony.

They were quickly caught and thrown in prison. Beatrice, Lucrezia and her older brother, Giacomo, were sentenced to death. Her 12-year-old brother, Bernardo, was forced to watch as his sister and stepmother were beheaded and his brother was drawn and quartered. Legend has it that every year on the anniversary of her death Beatrice returns to the bridge upon which she was executed, carrying her severed head.

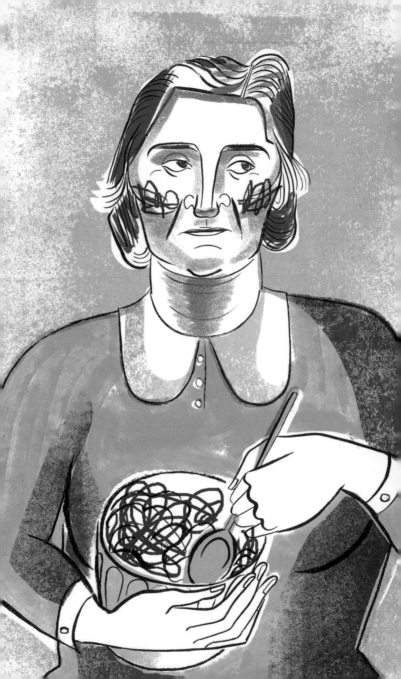

LEONARDA CIANCIULLI

Date of birth: 1893
Location: Italy
Date of murders: 1939–1940
Methodology: Axe
Penalty: 30 years in a criminal asylum

Fortune teller and matchmaker, Leonarda Cianciulli, was a superstitious woman. A psychic had told her that all her children would die in infancy, and indeed of 17 pregnancies, only three survived. When her son enlisted in the army, Cianciulli decided human sacrifices were required to protect him.

Her first victim was a spinster neighbour. After drugging her and chopping her up with an axe, Cianciulli drained out her blood, dried it in the oven and mixed it into a teacake batter, serving it to her son and friends. A second neighbour met a similarly bloody end. Cianciulli's third victim was a singer, Virginia Cacioppo. This time Cianciulli was even more creative about the body's disposal. From her memoirs: *She ended up in the pot, like the other two... her flesh was fat and white. When it had melted I added a bottle of cologne, and after a long time on the boil I was able to make some most acceptable creamy soap. I gave bars to neighbours and acquaintances. The cakes too were better: that woman was really sweet.*

Cacioppo's family alerted the police to her mysterious disappearance. Cianciulli was swiftly tracked down and readily confessed to the crimes, showing little remorse.

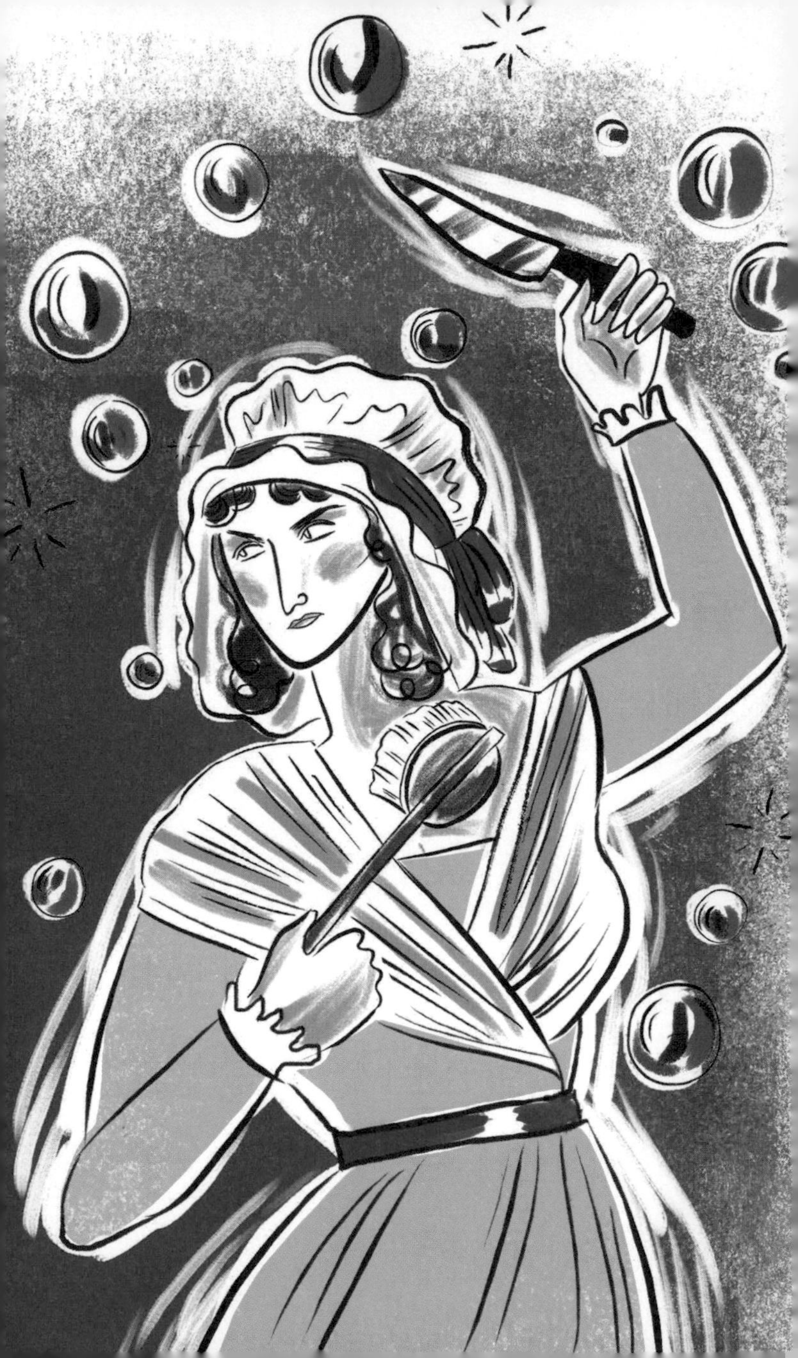

CHARLOTTE CORDAY

Date of birth: 1768
Location: France
Date of murder: 1793
Methodology: Stabbing
Penalty: Death by guillotine

Growing up in revolutionary France, Charlotte Corday aligned herself with the political philosophies of the Girodins. The Girodins offered a more moderate approach to the revolution than than their rivals, the Jacobins, who were at the time violently purging France of all royalist tendencies.

Jean-Paul Marat was a powerful voice of the Jacobin faction; writing incendiary calls-to-arms in his paper, *L'Ami du peuple*. Corday hatched a plan to assassinate him, believing that his death would bring an end to the violence and potentially save France from civil war. She initially planned to slaughter Marat in front of the entire National Convention, however, Marat had a painful skin condition that meant he had to spend most of his time at home in the bath. Corday encountered him there, gave him a list of Girodin 'traitors', and then plunged a knife into his chest.

At her trial, four days later, Corday stated, "I knew that Marat was perverting France. I have killed one man to save a hundred thousand". She was executed by guillotine. Afterwards, the Jacobins autopsied her body to find out whether she had been having an affair with a man who had masterminded the plan. She was found to be a virgin.

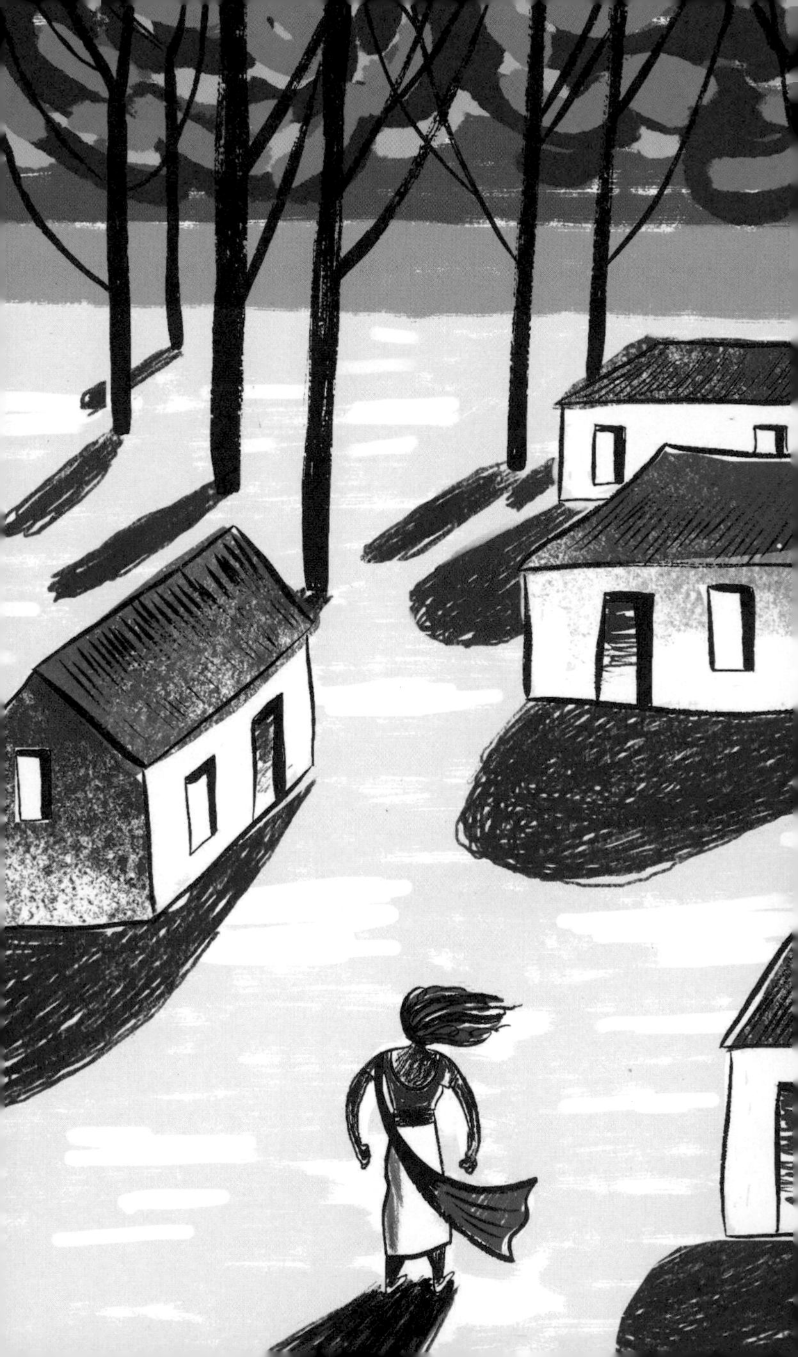

PHOOLAN DEVI

Date of birth: 1963
Location: India
Date of murders: 1981
Methodology: Shooting
Penalty: 11 year sentence

Phoolan Devi was born into a low-caste family in a rural Indian village. At the age of 11, she was married off to an older man who abused her. She escaped his family home and returned to her village, where she lived as an outcast until, at the age of 16, she was abducted by a gang of bandits. Phoolan fell in love with the leader of the gang, Vikram Mallah, and rose through the ranks, becoming a respected bandit queen.

However, divisions began to arise between higher and lower caste members in the gang. Eventually there was a mutiny, and Vikram Mallah was killed. Phoolan was abducted and taken to the village of Behmai, home of some of the upper-caste members, where she was gang raped for a period of three weeks. With help from her bandit allies, Phoolan managed to escape and formed a new gang. Seven months later, she returned to Behmai with her gang, lined up the men of the village and shot them all.

Phoolan then went on the run, protected by lower caste people who saw her as a heroic Robin Hood-type. She surrendered two years later and served 11 years in prison. She was released in 1996 and went on to have a career in politics. In 2001 she was shot dead in revenge for the Behmai massacre.

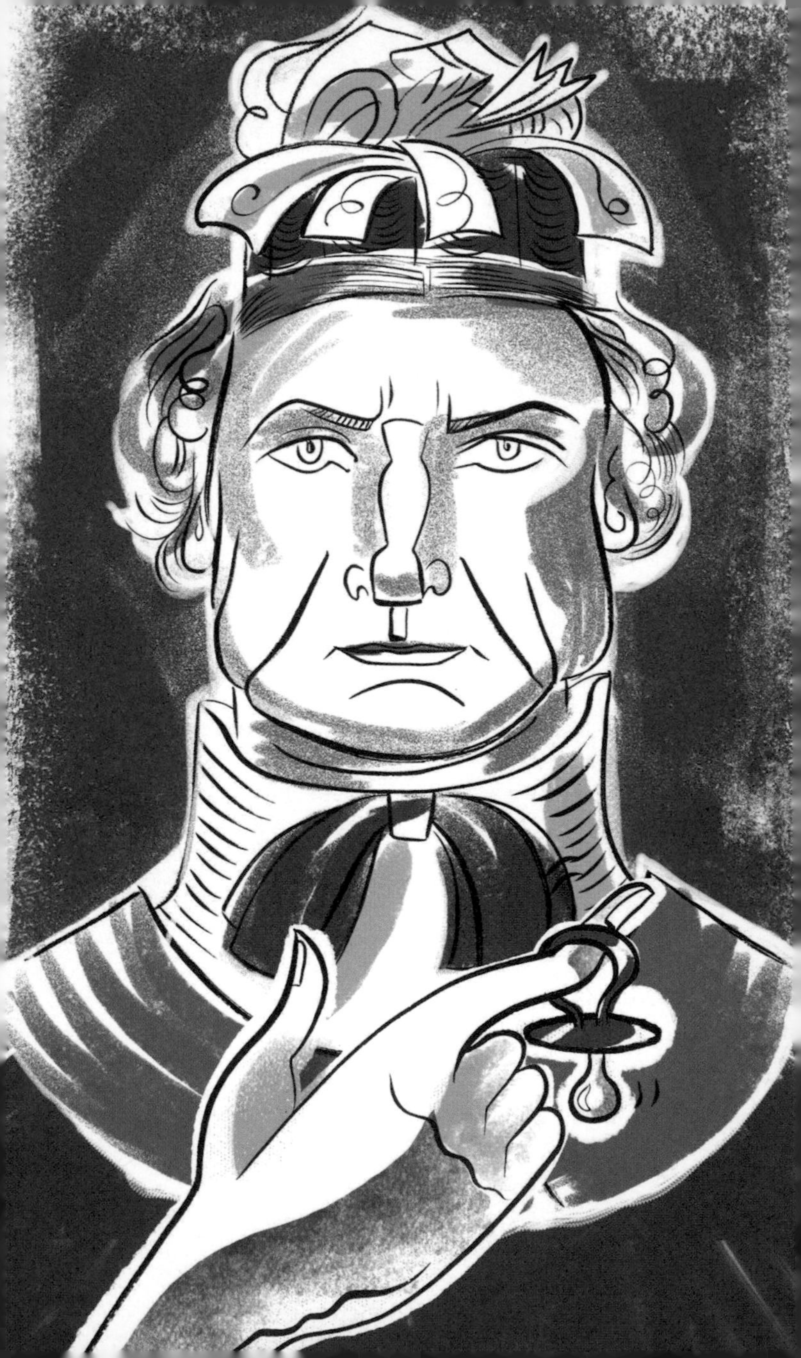

AMELIA ELIZABETH DYER

Date of birth: 1839
Location: England
Date of murders: 1880–1896
Methodology: Strangulation
Penalty: Death by hanging

Victorian attitudes to unmarried mothers were unforgiving; fathers were not obliged to pay maintenance, and the disgraced women would be barred from working and often forced into prostitution and penury. Capitalising on this state of affairs, Amelia Dyer was one of many 'baby farmers' who would charge a fee to relieve women of unwanted babies.

Initially, Dyer followed the methods of her contemporaries, and 'fostered' the children, generally neglecting them or drugging them with opiates until they died. However, after serving a six-month term for child neglect, Dyer changed her modus operandi. Rather than fostering, she filed advertisements in which she would pitch herself as a respectable, married woman who could offer a secure future for the unwanted baby in return for a hefty one-off fee. Within hours of receiving the babies, she would strangle them using a length of white tape and dump their bodies in the Thames.

Amelia Dyer was eventually caught when one of the bodies was discovered wrapped in paper marked with her address. She was arrested in connection with two child murders, but it is thought that she was actually responsible for the deaths of around 400 babies. She was sentenced to hang.

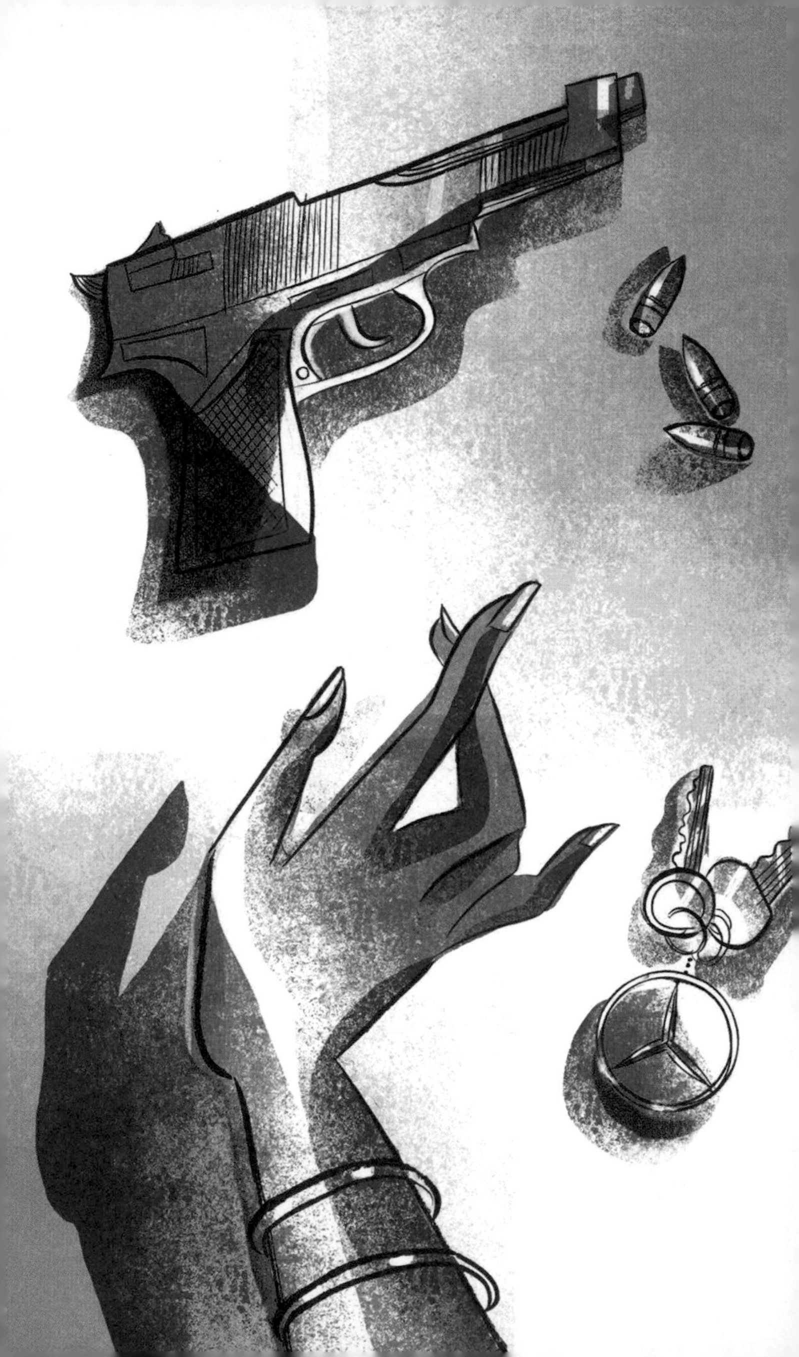

MONA FANDEY

Date of birth: 1966
Location: Malaysia
Date of murder: 1993
Methodology: Axe
Penalty: Death by hanging

Mona Fandey was born Maznah Ismail, but changed her name in the late '70s, when she launched an unsuccessful pop career. After leaving the music business, Fandey reinvented herself as a *bomoh*, a witch doctor, promising local dignitaries and aristocrats amulets and spells for protection and wealth.

In 1993, ambitious local politician, Datuk Mazlan Idris, came seeking her services. In return for a princely sum, Fandey proposed a cleansing ritual, which would help him in his political aspirations. Idris was asked to lie on the floor with his eyes closed and wait for money to fall from the sky. Fandey's assistant then swiftly chopped his head off with an axe, and Fandey, her assistant and her husband all worked together to skin Idris, chop him into pieces and bury him. The morning after the murder, Fandey went to the mall and bought herself a Mercedes and a facelift.

Fandey and her accomplices were swiftly tracked down and a much-publicised trial began. The flamboyant Fandey seemed to take great pleasure in the resulting attention, smiling, posing and commenting "looks like I still have many fans". She was hanged in 2001 and her last words were "I will never die".

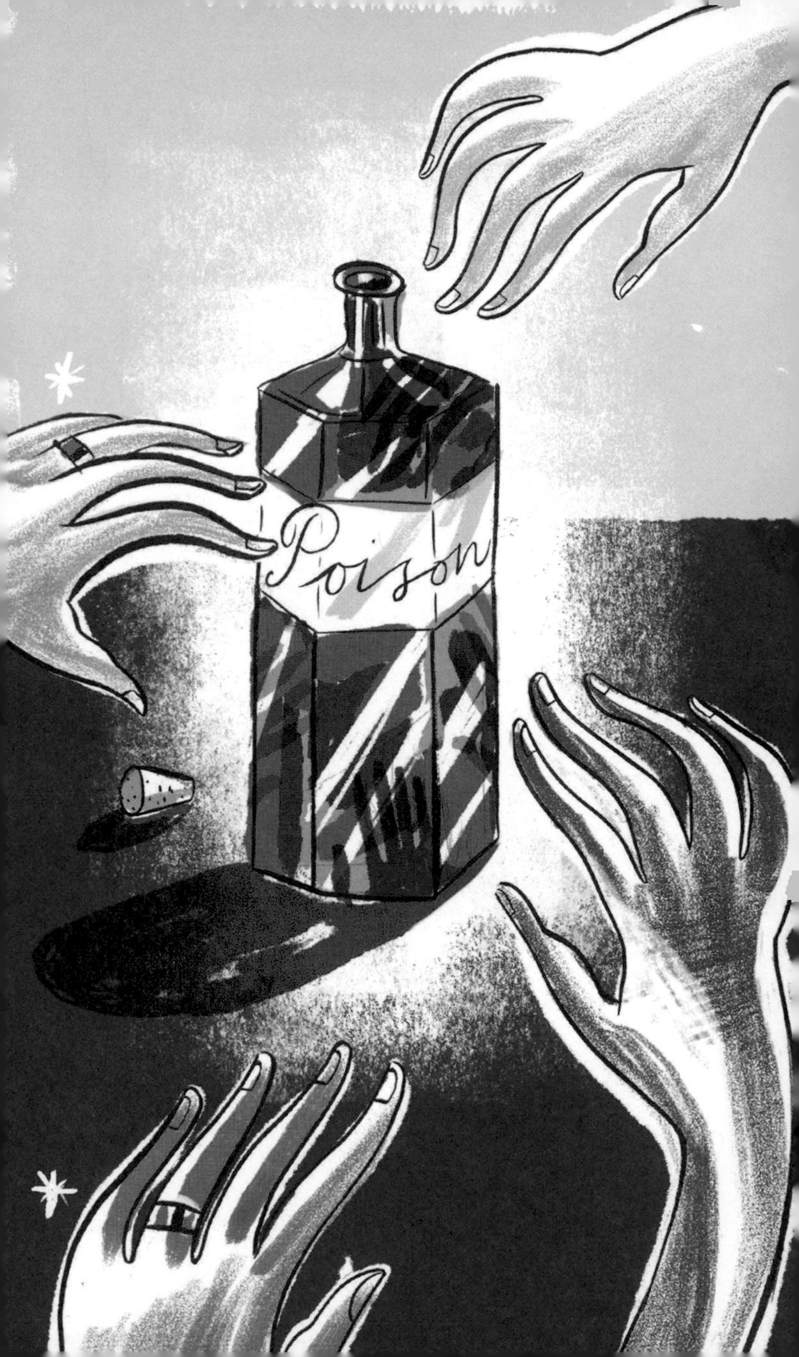
Poison

JULIA FAZEKAS AND THE ANGEL MAKERS OF NAGYREV

Date of birth: Unknown
Location: Hungary
Date of murders: 1911–1929
Methodology: Poison
Status: Death by suicide

Julia Fazekas was a midwife who appeared in the small rural village of Nagyrev in 1911 and quickly established herself as a wise-woman/doctor/abortionist. When the First World War broke out, the village became a holding location for prisoners of war. Whilst the men of the village were away fighting, many women, freshly liberated from their often-abusive husbands, took POW lovers.

When the men found their way back from the battlefields, their wives were loathe to return to their old ways of life and turned to Fazekas for help. Fazekas boiled up a load of flypaper, extracting the arsenic, and sold bottles of it to the women, who sprinkled it on their husbands' dinners. Once they had disposed of their husbands, many of the women went on to eliminate other cumbersome family members; elderly parents, lovers and even children. Between 1911 and 1929 at least 50 murders occurred in Nagyrev.

In 1929, an anonymous tip-off to the press alerted the authorities to the situation. Corpses were exhumed and as the truth emerged, many of the women confessed. 38 were arrested, eight were sentenced to death and the rest received prison sentences. It is thought that Fazekas took her own life.

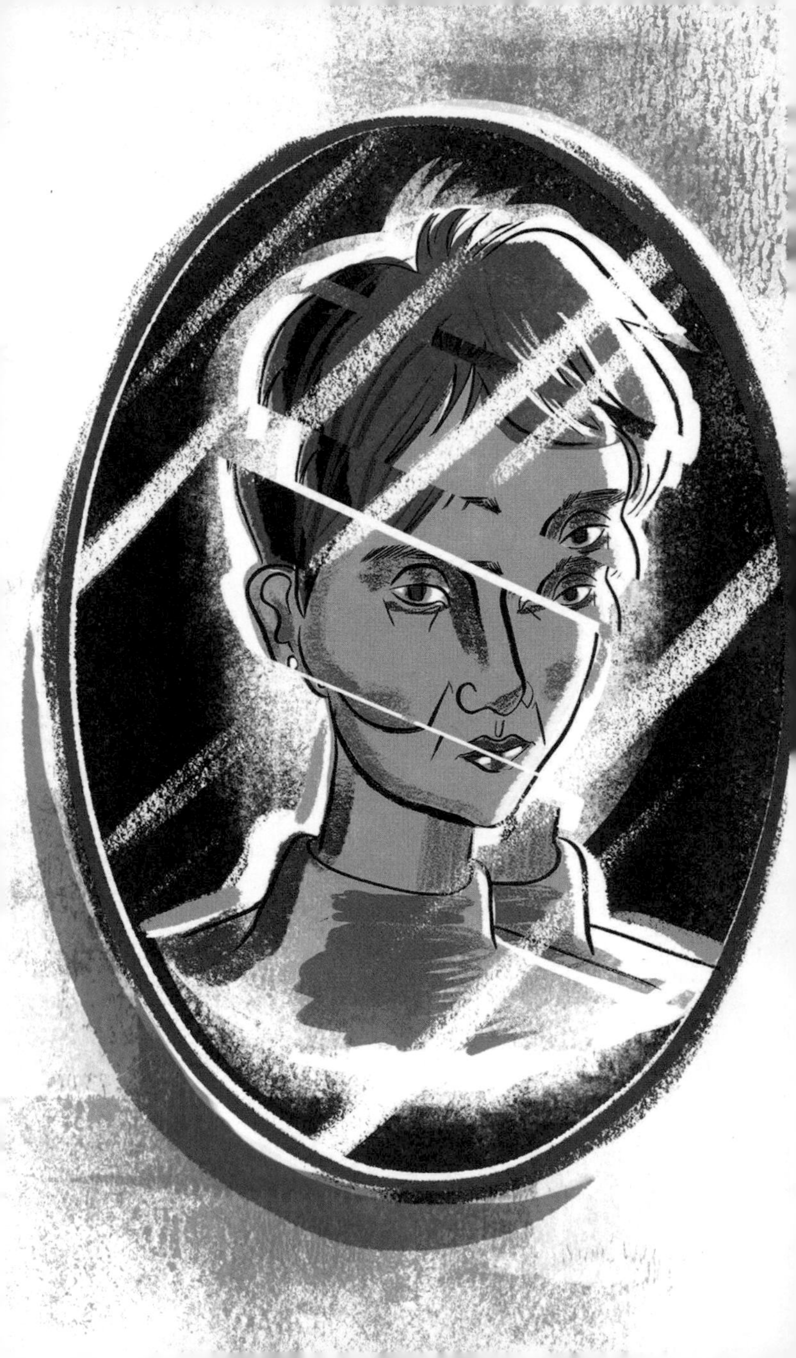

GU KAILAI

Date of birth: 1958
Location: China
Date of murder: 2011
Methodology: Poison
Penalty: Sentenced to life

Gu Kailai was born into a prominent communist family. She married Bo Xilai, an influential politician, and the two were one of China's most high-flying couples. However, in 2012, their fortunes were upended when an assistant to Bo implicated Gu in the murder of British businessman, Neil Heywood.

Gu's trial lasted only one day, and Chinese authorities kept a tight lock on media coverage in the courtroom. According to Chinese media, Gu poisoned Heywood when he attempted to blackmail her following a botched business deal. Gu confessed and was given a life sentence.

However, various international media outlets investigated further. It became apparent that rather than a deal gone wrong, Heywood had been laundering hundreds of millions of dollars for Gu and Bo and had demanded a larger cut for his efforts. In a further twist, when footage did eventually emerge from the trial, it seemed that the woman in the dock was not Gu Kailai. Significantly different facial features indicated that a body double had stood trial, and was presumably serving time. Despite the international outrage at the way the case was handled, it was never re-examined.

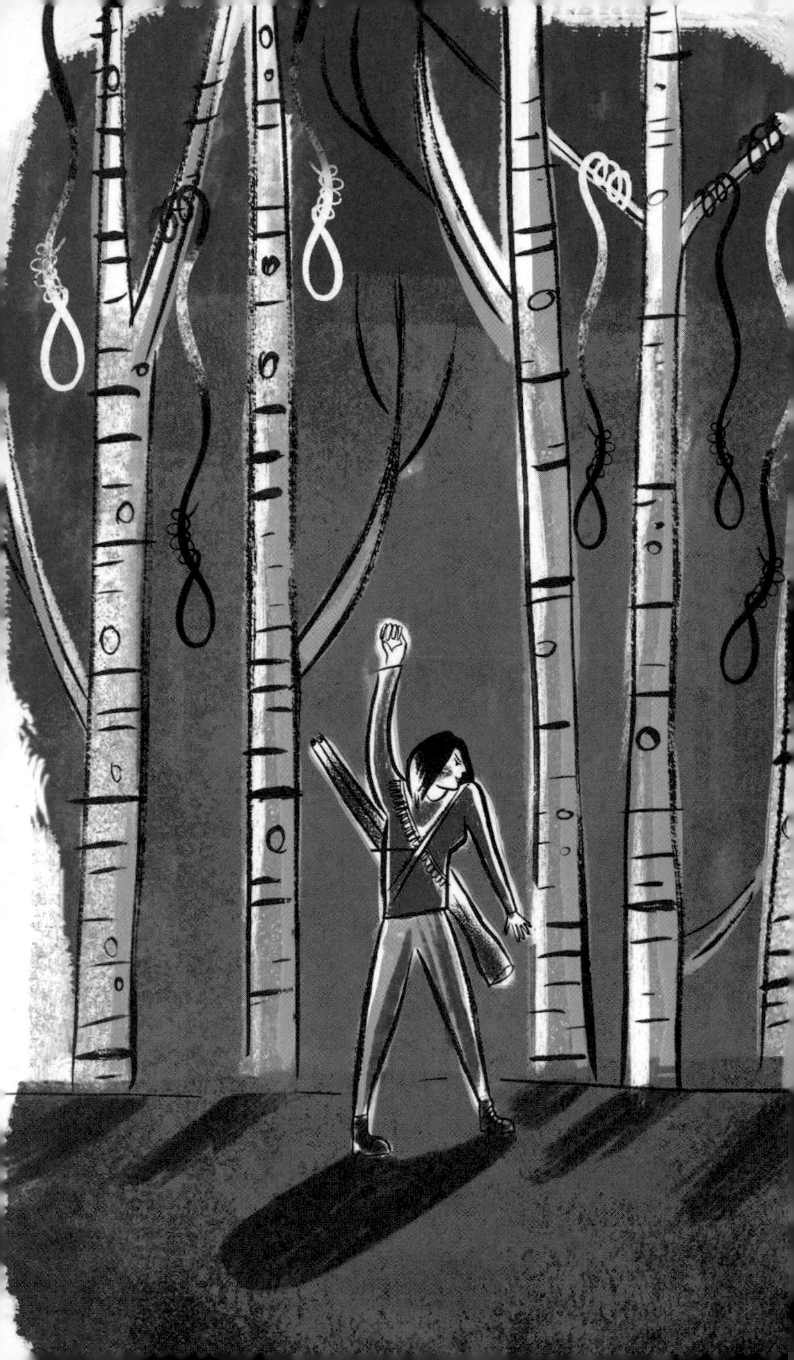

HIROKO NAGATA

Date of birth: 1945
Location: Japan
Date of murders: 1971-1972
Methodology: Battery and torture
Penalty: Sentenced to death

Hiroko Nagata became involved in radical left wing politics during her time at university. Joining forces with fellow student, Tsuneo Mori, she co-led a Marxist faction called the United Red Army (URA). She was known for her vicious temper, and when in August 1971, two members of the group tried to defect, she was instrumental in their lynching. Their bodies were buried in the nearby marshes.

A few months later, the police cracked down on the group, and Nagata and 29 other members of the URA fled to a remote mountain compound. Whilst there, Nagata and Mori initiated 'self examination' sessions, which evolved into the lynchings of members who were not deemed sufficiently revolutionary. Eight members and one non-member were beaten to death for taking too much interest in sexual relations. Six further members caught trying to escape were tied to trees and left to freeze to death.

The paramilitary put an end to the bloodbath in February, 1972. Nagata was arrested and sentenced to death. She died in prison of a brain tumour in 2011, still awaiting her execution.

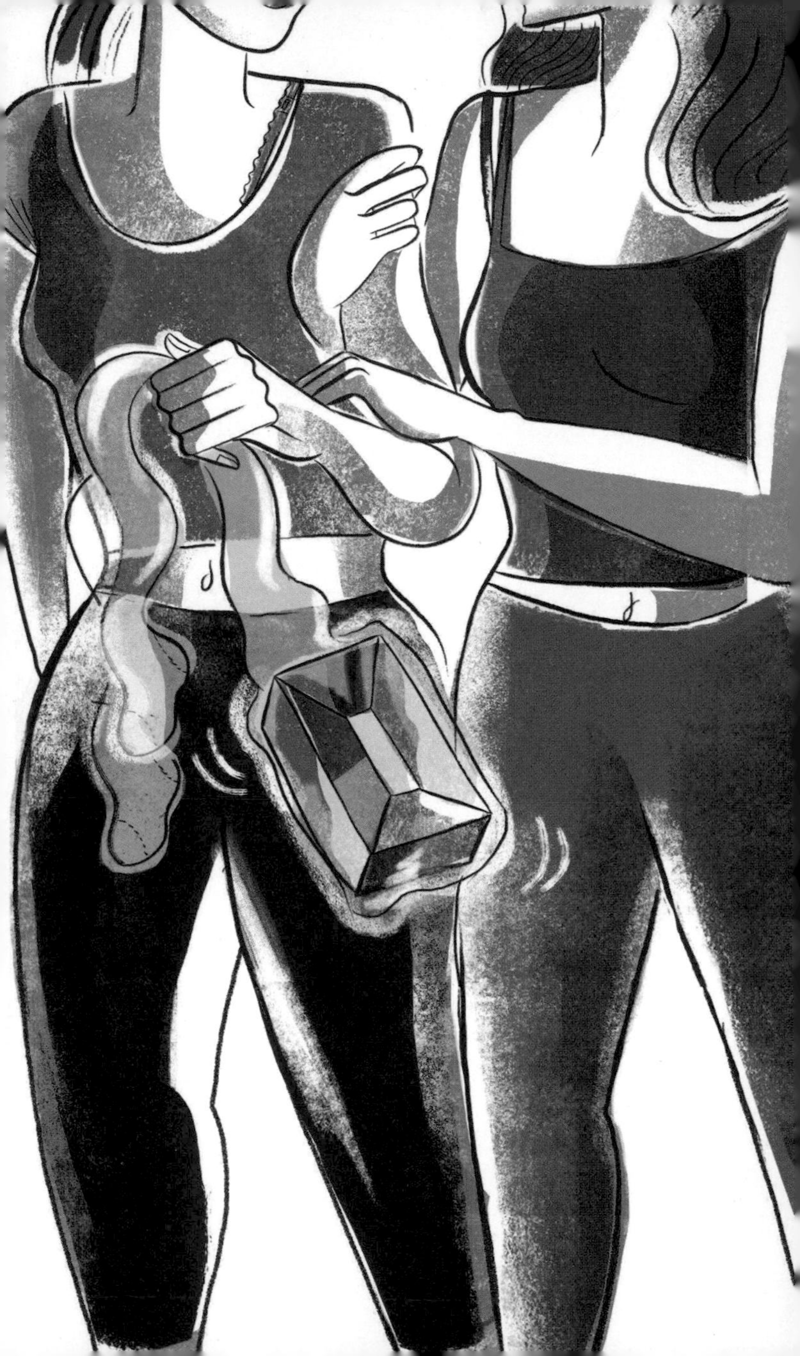

PAULINE PARKER & JULIET HULME

Dates of birth: 1935 and 1936 respectively
Location: New Zealand
Date of murder: 1954
Methodology: Battery
Penalty: Served five years in prison

Pauline Parker and Juliet Hulme met as teenagers in Christchurch. Despite their different backgrounds, they bonded over a mutual love of opera and formed an intense friendship. Together they created an elaborate fantasy world filled with heroes, villains and dreams of Hollywood stardom.

Their parents disapproved of the relationship, which they feared was sexual. Juliet's father decided to send his daughter to stay with his sister in South Africa, implying to Juliet that Pauline could go with her. Pauline's mother, Honorah, predictably said this was out of the question, and the girls hatched a plan to kill her. Whilst on a walk, Juliet dropped a stone, and when Honorah bent to pick it up, Pauline smashed her over the head with a brick inside a stocking. The intention was for Honorah to die straight away so they could make it look like a fall, but in actuality the stocking broke and the girls took turns holding Honorah down and clubbing her to death with the brick.

Their story of accidental death quickly fell apart and the girls each served around five years in prison. They both assumed new identities and moved separately to the United Kingdom. Hulme pursued a successful career as a crime writer.

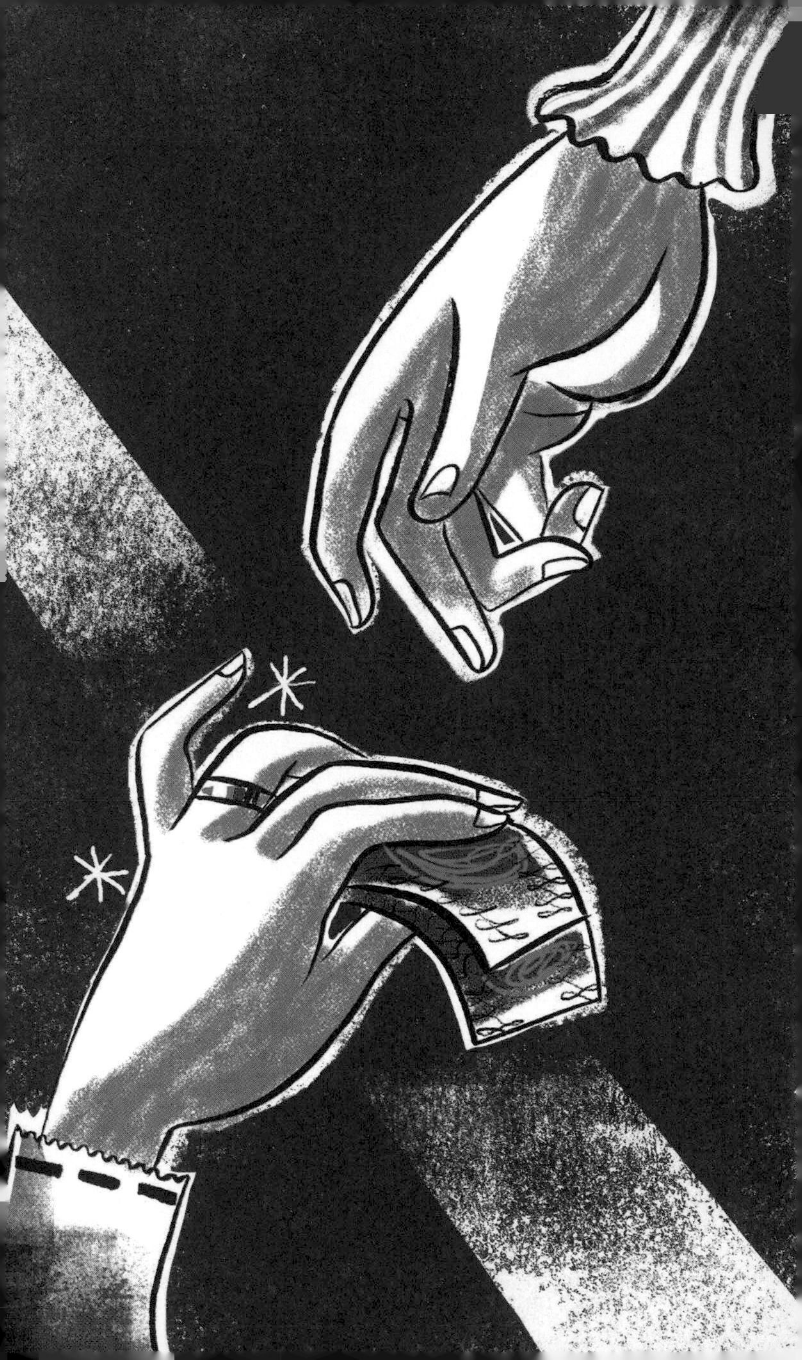

MADAME POPOVA

Date of birth: Unknown
Location: Russia
Date of murders: 1879-1909
Methodology: Poisoning
Penalty: Death by firing squad

Madame Popova ran a small disposal service for women who wanted to be freed of their abusive husbands. Promising complete secrecy and charging a nominal fee in return for what she saw as a charitable service, Popova's business was soon bustling. Her method was simple, she would gain the trust of her victim, and then either she or an assistant would slip lethal poison into his food or drink.

Popova continued in this way for about 30 years, until eventually one of her clients, wracked with remorse for her husband's murder, turned her into the police. When collecting her from her home, police had to evade a huge angry mob, demanding that Popova be burned at the stake.

Once in custody, Popova showed little remorse. She boasted that she had done "excellent work liberating 300 unhappy wives from their tyrants", and stated in her defense that she had "never once killed a woman". Popova refused to divulge the names of her assistants or her many clients and was executed by firing squad, unrepentant.

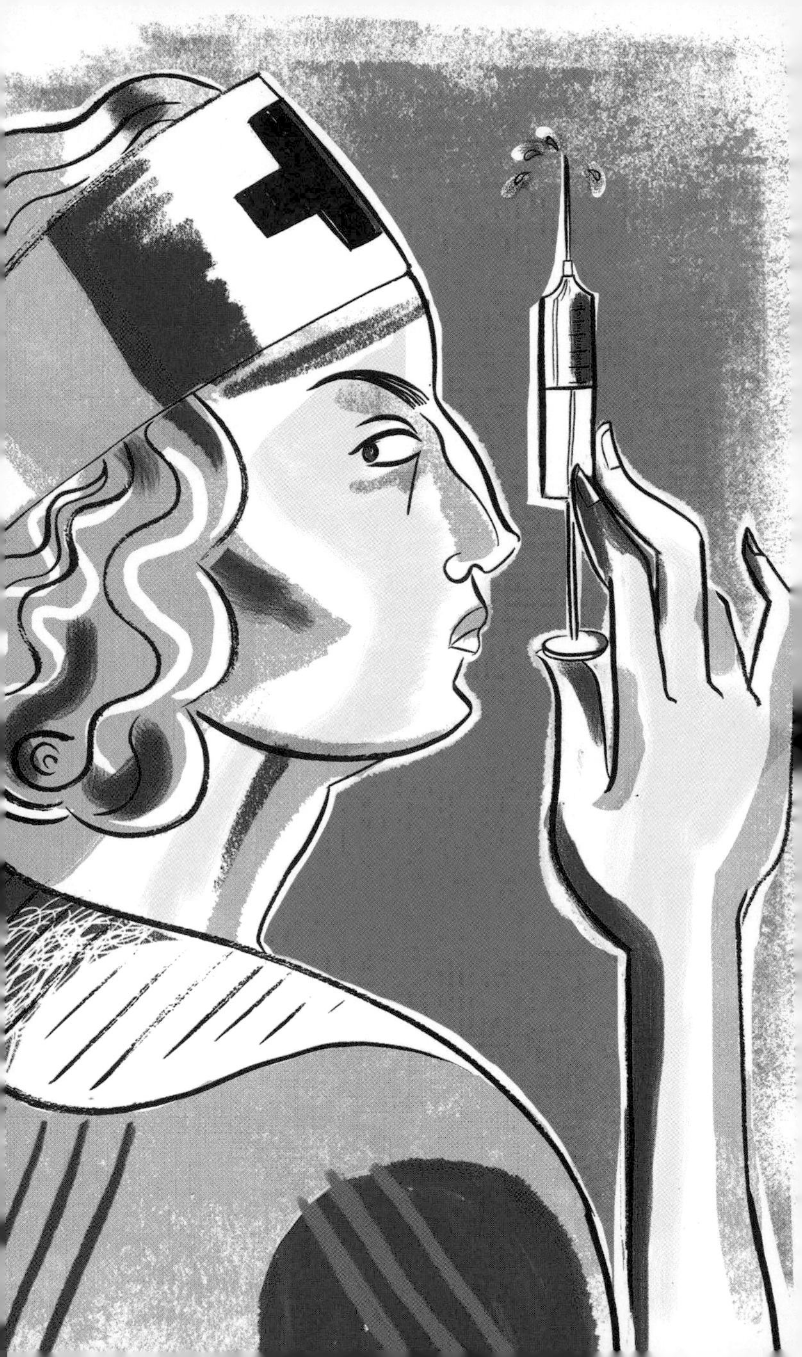

WALTRAUD WAGNER
AND THE LAINZ ANGELS OF DEATH

Date of birth: 1960
Location: Austria
Date of murders: 1983-1989
Methodology: Drugging and drowning
Penalty: Sentenced to life

Waltraud Wagner worked as a nurse's aid in a hospital ward for older and unruly patients in the Vienna suburb of Lainz. In 1983, an elderly patient asked Wagner to end her life. Wagner did so, injecting her with an overdose of morphine, and found that the power it gave her was intoxicating.

She confided in three other nurses; Maria Gruber, Irene Leidolf and Stephanjia Meyer, and the four women were soon regularly injecting difficult patients with lethal doses of drugs. After a while, their approach became more sadistic; one woman would pinch the victim's nose whilst the other poured water in their mouth until they drowned. This method was both thrilling for the women to watch and was also hard to detect, as elderly patients frequently have water in their lungs. Within five years, somewhere between 50 and 200 patients were murdered. The hospital, which had been involved in exterminating elderly people in the Nazi era, stonewalled any investigation into to the high death rate.

The women were finally caught when a doctor overheard them joking about one of their victims in a bar. Wagner was convicted and merrily confessed: "The ones who got on my nerves were given a free bed with the good Lord". The women received lengthy sentences, but by 2008 all had been released.

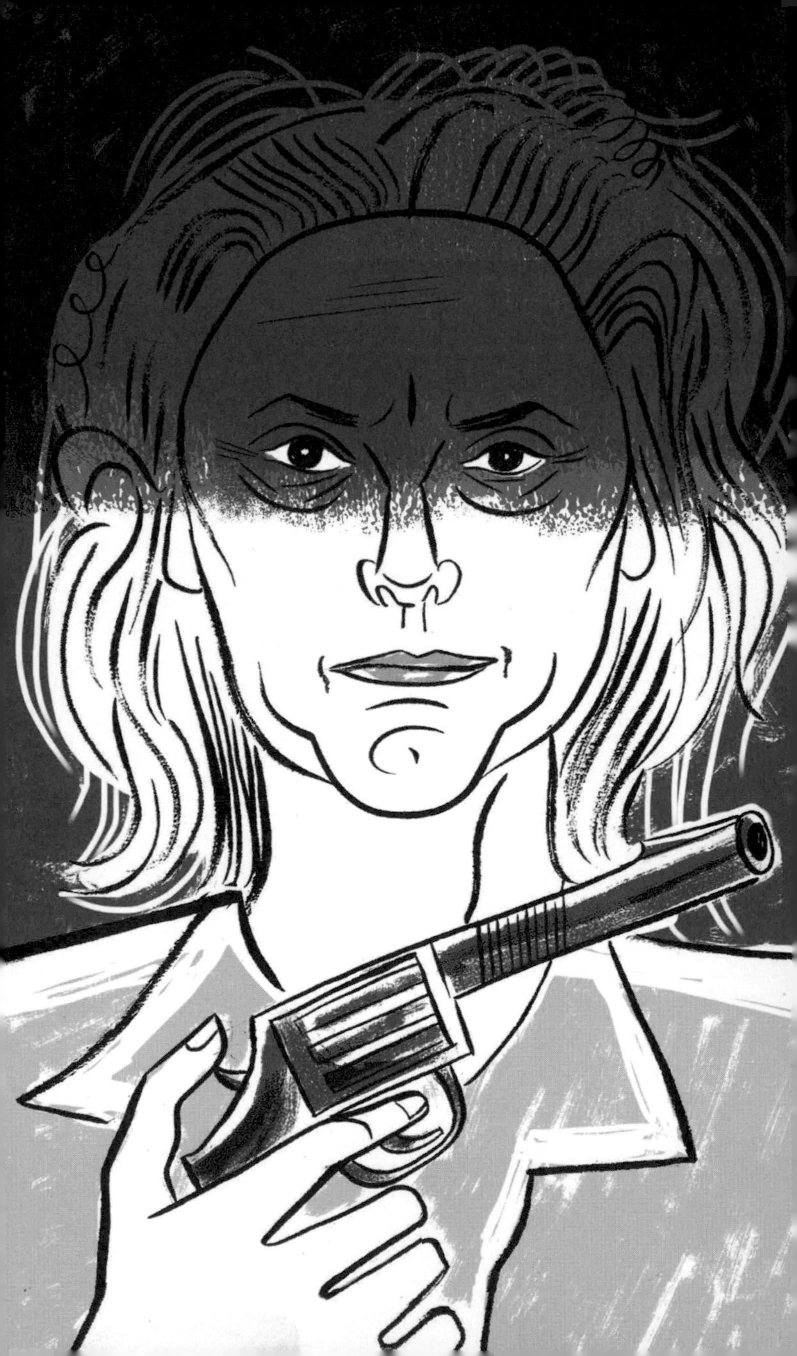

AILEEN WUORNOS

Date of birth: 1956
Location: USA
Date of murders: 1989–1990
Methodology: Shooting
Penalty: Death by lethal injection

Aileen Wuornos had a troubled childhood, fraught with sexual abuse and neglect. She was kicked out of her grandparents' home at the age of 15 and began supporting herself through prostitution. A life of escalating violence and criminal activity followed.

In 1987, Wuornos fell in love with a woman called Tyria Moore and the two moved in together, living off Wournos's prostition earnings. In 1989, Wournos was apparently raped by client (and convicted rapist) Richard Mallory, and shot him several times. A year-long shooting spree followed, in which Wuornos posed as a hitchhiker/sex worker, luring six more men to remote locations and shotting them with a .22 calibre pistol.

Wuornos was eventually arrested, and Moore agreed to testify against her in exchange for immunity. Despite Wuornos's obviously erratic behavior in court, and her insistence that all her victims had attempted to rape her, Wuornos was sentenced to death. Her story was recounted in a number of successful films, and she became something of a countercultural icon – a gay sex-worker with severe psychiatric issues, who was as much a victim of circumstance as a perpetrator. She professed her love for Moore until her dying day.

Published by Cicada Books Limited

Illustrated by Sarah Tanat-Jones
Written by Anna Davies
Design by April

British Library Cataloguing-in-Publication Data.

A CIP record for this book is available from
the British Library.
ISBN: 978-1-908714-41-1

Printed in China

CO

Cicada Books Limited
48 Burghley Road
London NW5 1UE
E: cicadabooks@gmail.com
W: www.cicadabooks.co.uk

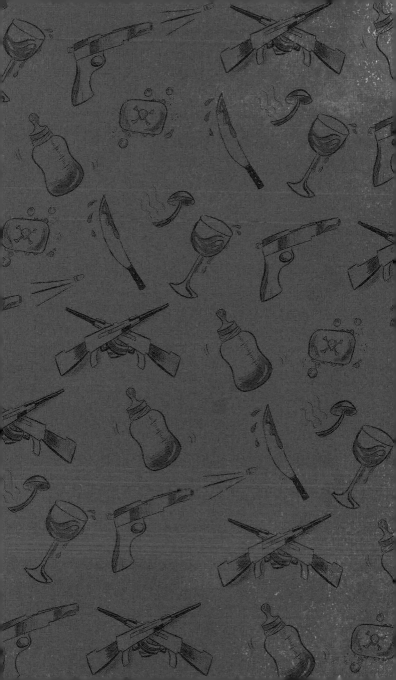

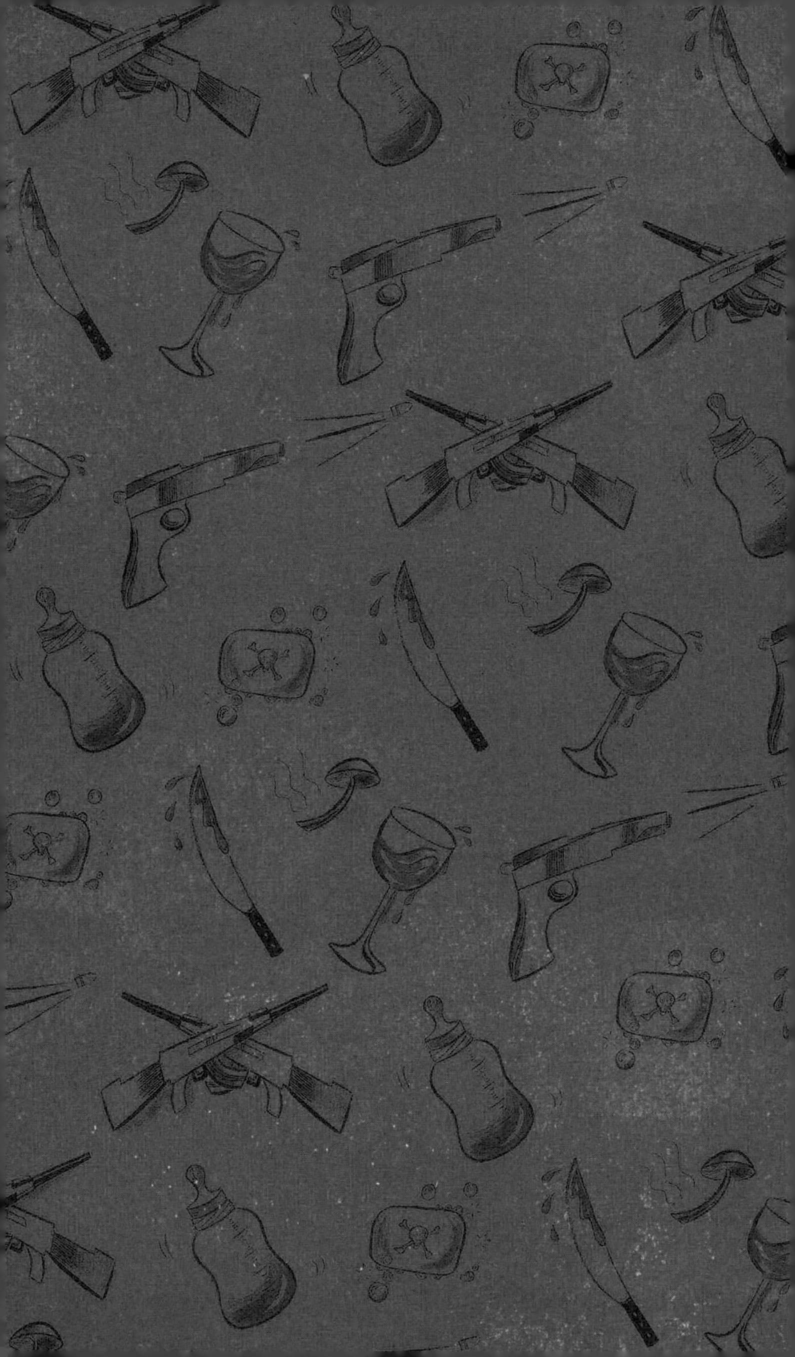